Doodle Design & Draw

ROCK STAR FASHIONS

Jennie Sun

DOVER PUBLICATIONS, INC.
Mineola, New York

Note

Over fifty fabulous and funky fashions need some finishing touches before they're ready for the rock and pop stars of Hollywood. Just grab a pencil and begin adding color, fabric patterns, accessories, and more, to the incomplete fashion designs. Featuring a series of illustrations right out of the coolest celebrity magazines, aspiring fashion designers will love testing their skills and creativity with *Doodle, Design & Draw—ROCK STAR FASHIONS*. The inside covers include sample fabric patterns for extra inspiration.

Bibliographical Note

Doodle, Design & Draw—ROCK STAR FASHIONS is a new work, first published by Dover Publications, Inc., in 2012.

International Standard Book Number

ISBN-13: 978-0-486-48703-8
ISBN-10: 0-486-48703-2

Manufactured in the United States by Courier Corporation
48703201
www.doverpublications.com

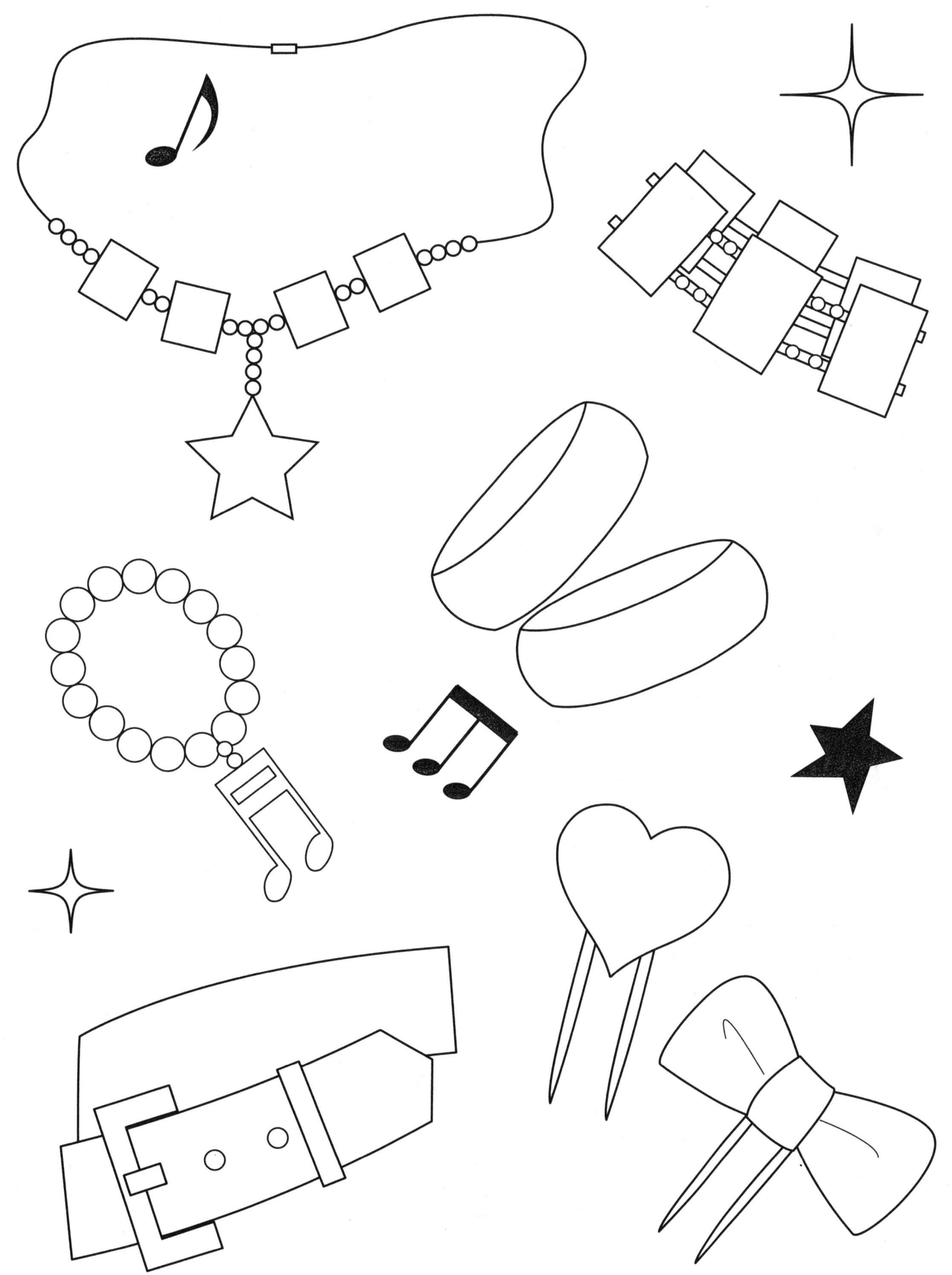

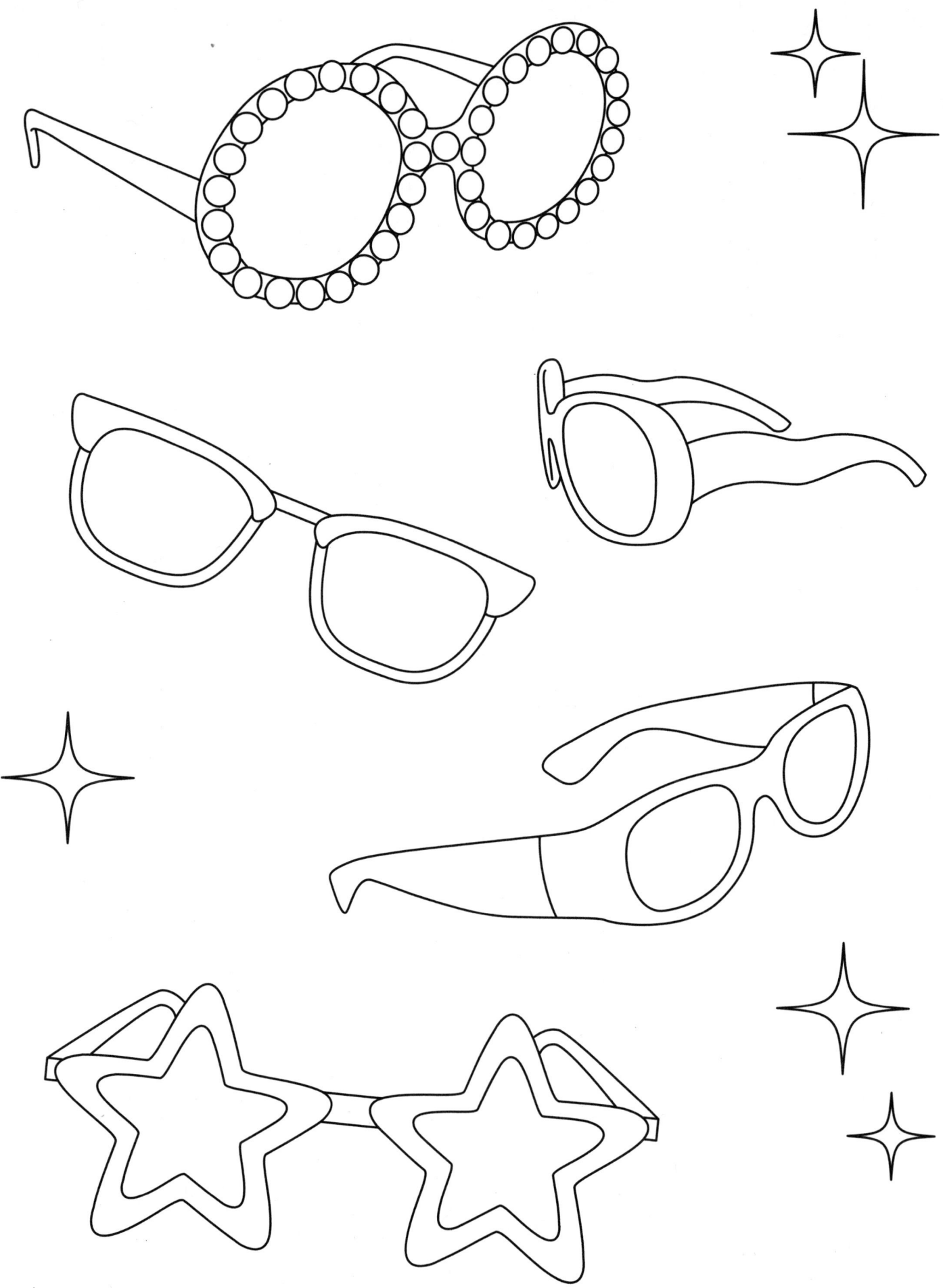

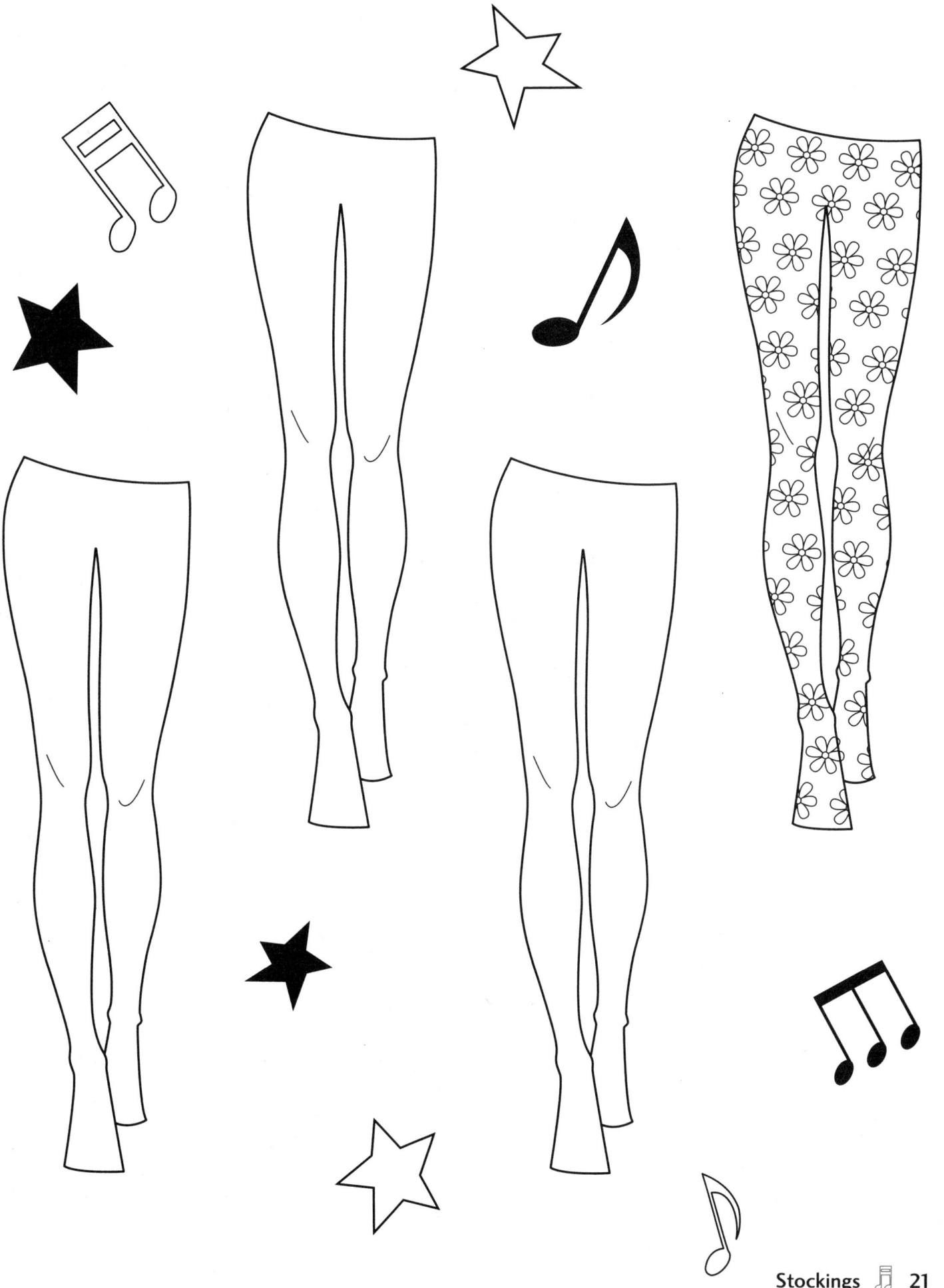

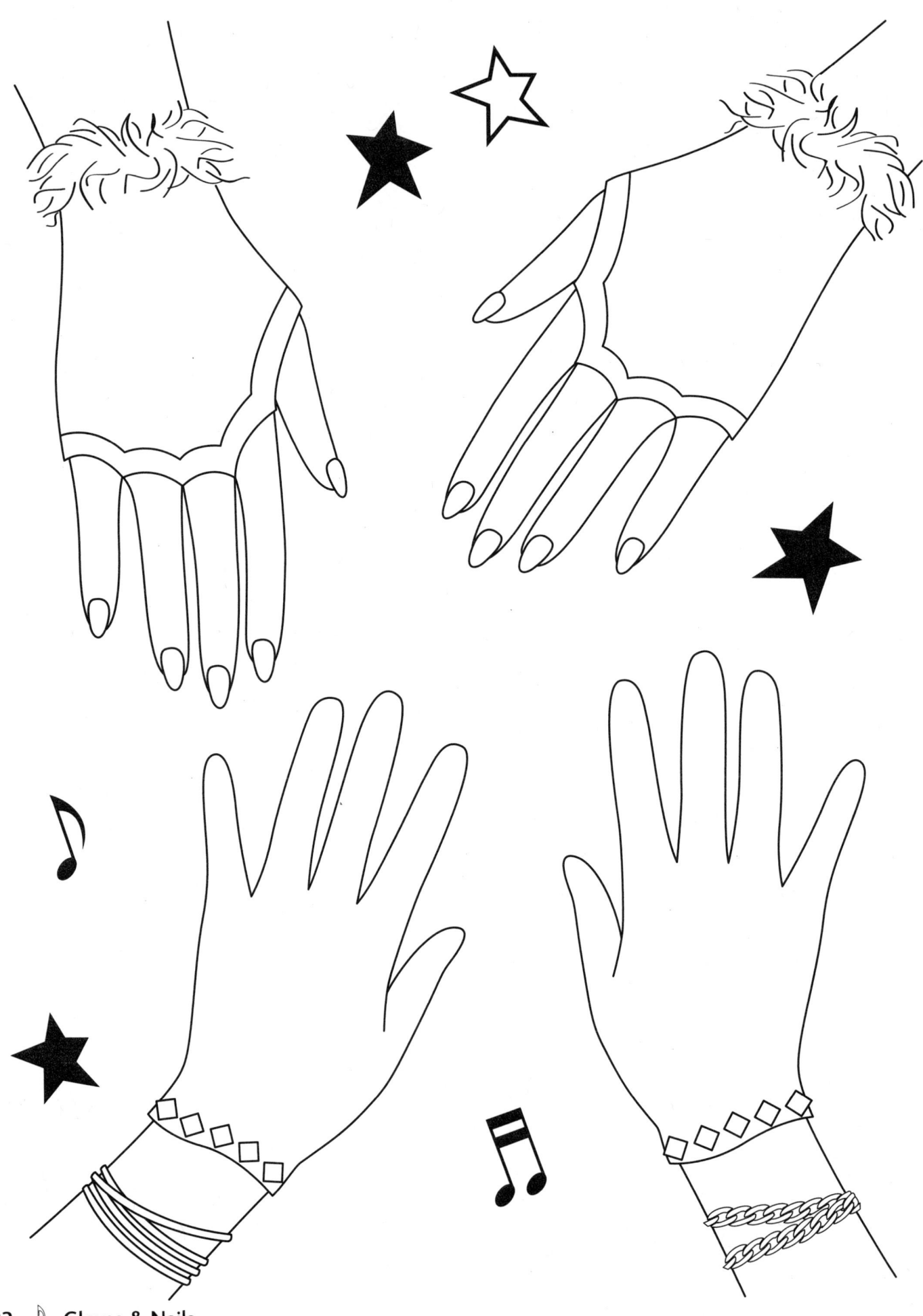

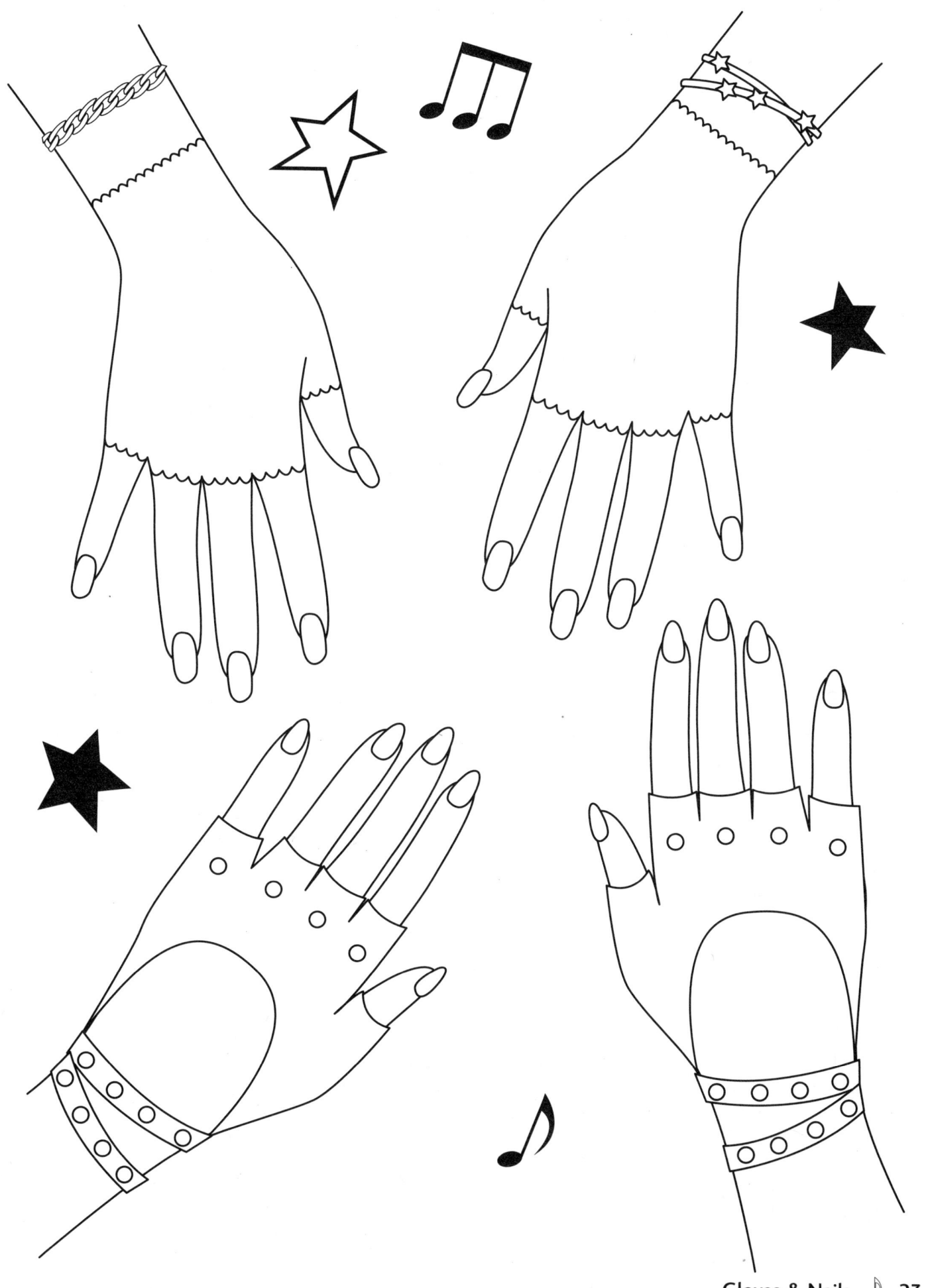

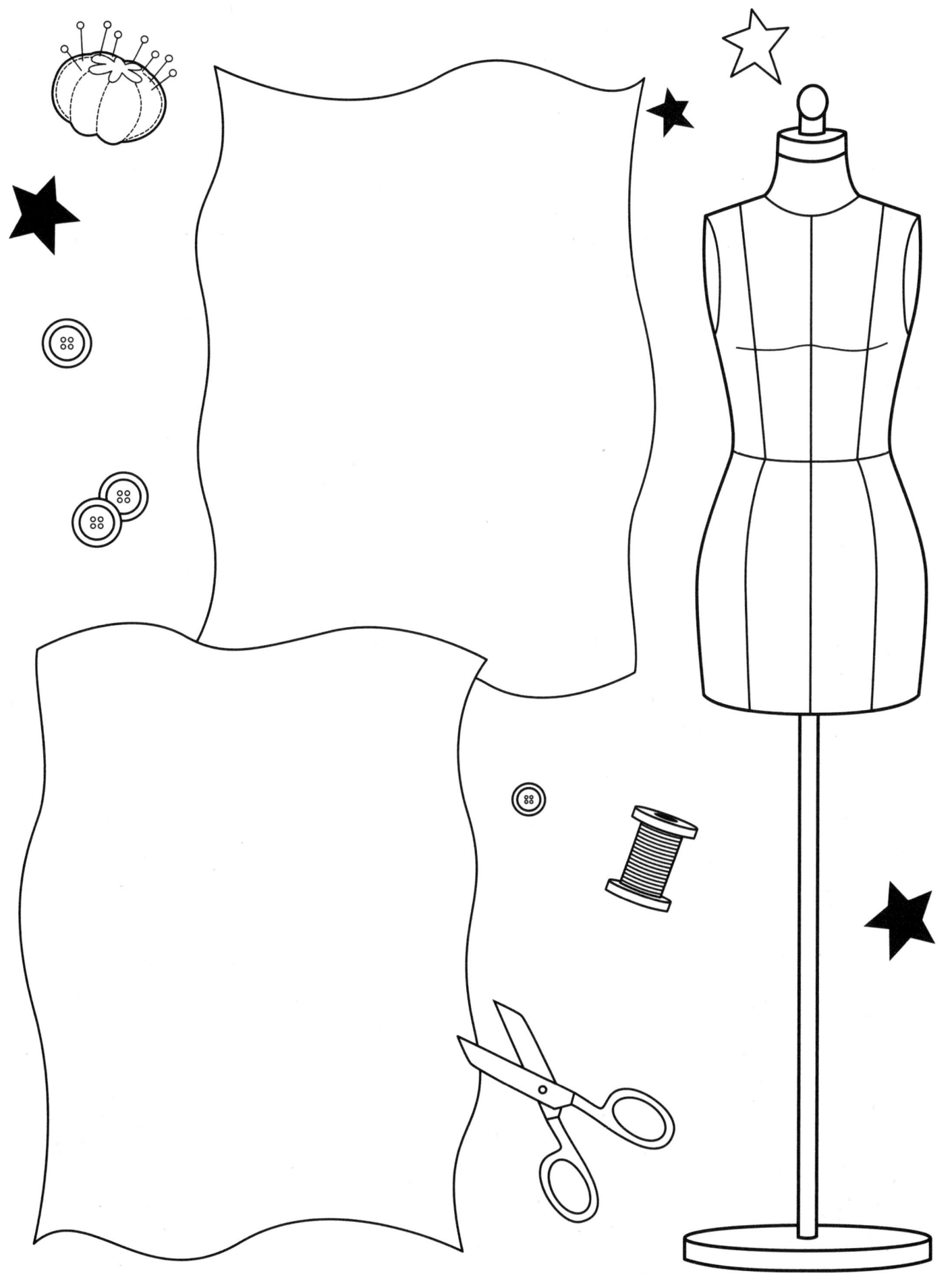

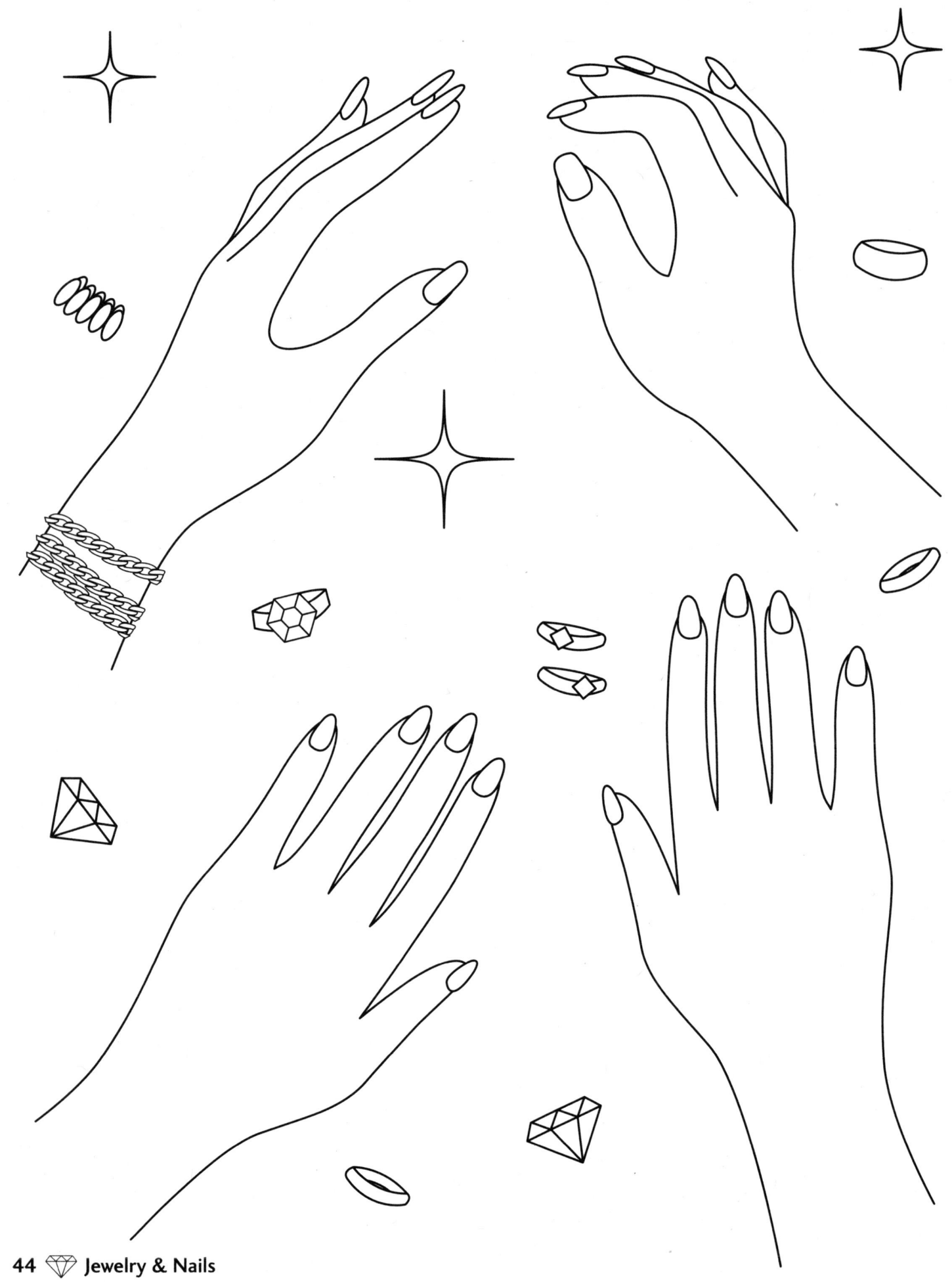

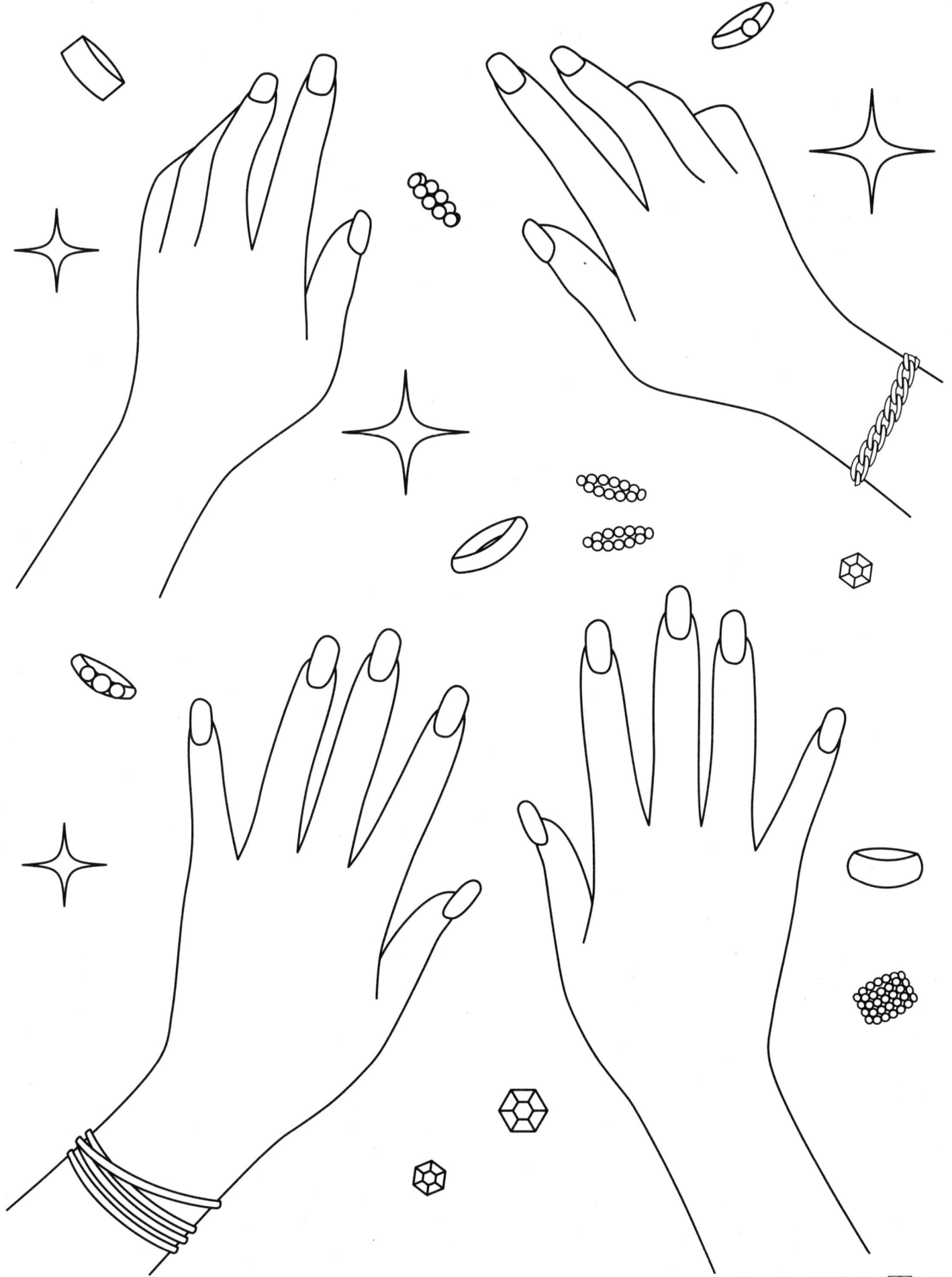

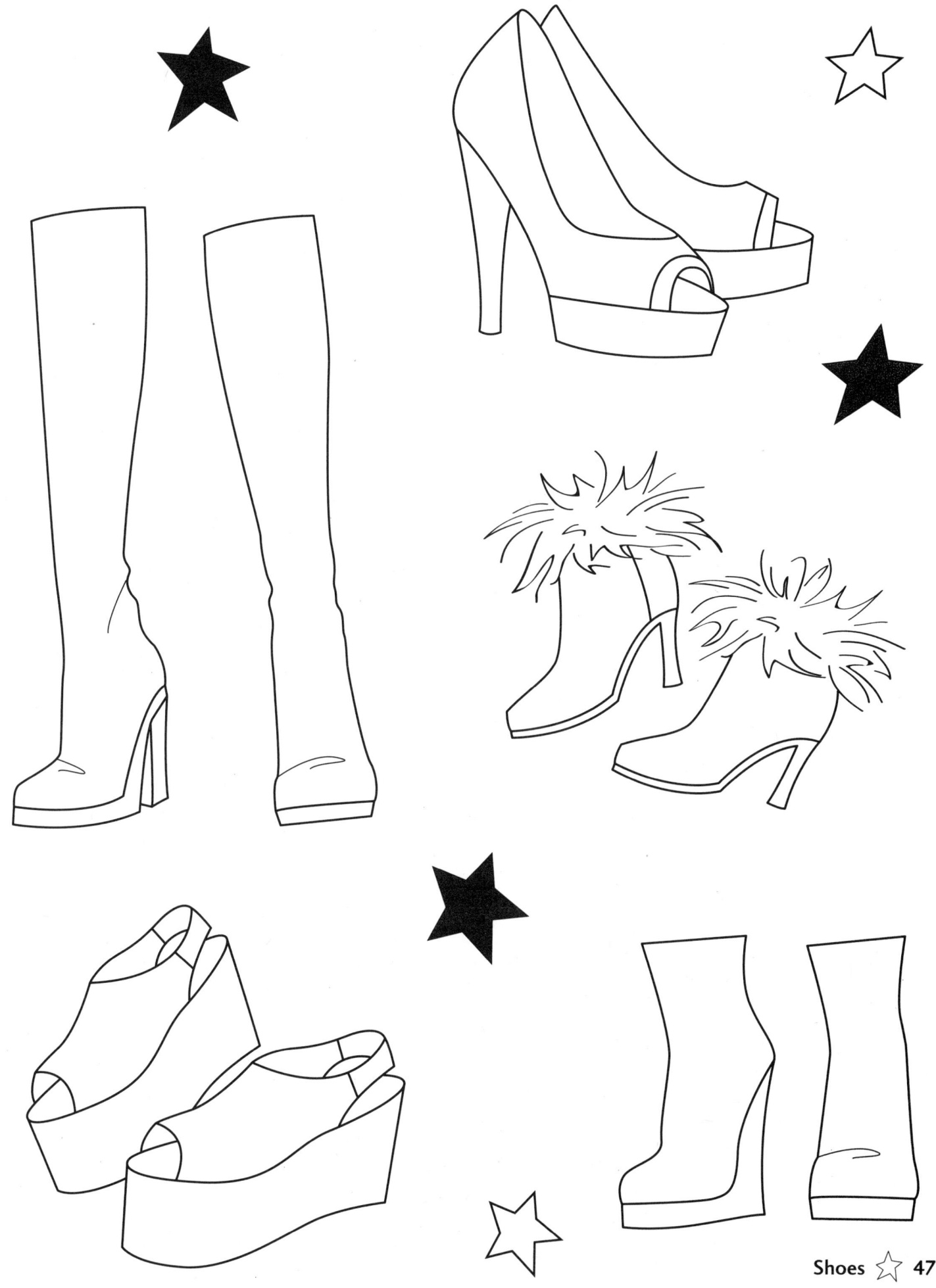

48 ♡ Concert

STAGE